HAUNTED! THE QUEEN MARY

Gareth Stevens
Publishing

BY THERESE SHEA

Please visit our website, www.garethstevens.com. For a free color catalog of all our high-quality books, call toll free 1-800-542-2595 or fax 1-877-542-2596.

Library of Congress Cataloging-in-Publication Data

Shea, Therese M.

Haunted! The Queen Mary / by Therese M. Shea.

   p. cm. — (History's most haunted)

Includes index.

ISBN 978-1-4339-9259-9 (pbk.)

ISBN 978-1-4339-9260-5 (6-pack)

ISBN 978-1-4339-9258-2 (library binding)

1. Ghosts—Pacific Coast (U.S.)—Juvenile literature. 2. Queen Mary (Steamship)—Miscellanea. I. Title.

BF1486.S24 2014

133.122—dc23

First Edition

Published in 2014 by
Gareth Stevens Publishing
111 East 14th Street, Suite 349
New York, NY 10003

Copyright © 2014 Gareth Stevens Publishing

Designer: Nicholas Domiano
Editor: Kristen Rajczak

Photo credits: Cover, p. 1 jan kranendonk/Shutterstock.com; p. 5 Topical Press Agency/Hulton Archive/Getty Images; pp. 6, 10 Keystone/Hulton Archive/Getty Images; p. 7 Planet News Archive/SSPL/Getty Images; p. 9 Florian Boyd/Wikimedia Commons; p. 11 Time & Life Pictures/US Coast Guard/Time & Life Pictures/ Getty Images; p. 13. Central Press/Hulton Archive/Getty Images; p. 15 Leemage/Universal Image Group/ Getty Images; p. 17 Fox Photos/Hulton Archive/Getty Images; p. 19 Photoshot/Hulton Archive/Getty Images; p. 20 Zachary/Wikimedia Commons; p. 21 Common Good/Wikimedia Commons; pp. 22–23, 25 Science & Society Picture Library/SSPL/Getty Images; p. 27 Hudson/Hulton Archive/Getty Images; p. 29 Thomas McConville/Photographer's Choice/Getty Images.

Printed in the United States of America

CPSIA compliance information: Batch #CS13GS: For further information contact Gareth Stevens, New York, New York at 1-800-542-2595.

CONTENTS

Words in the glossary appear in **bold** type the first time they are used in the text.

SPOOKY SHIP

Have you ever seen a figure appear or disappear in front of your eyes? Have you heard voices in an empty room? Even if you haven't, many people say they have. Some unexplained events make us wonder if ghosts really do exist. Certain places seem to have more unexplained **phenomena** than others, and so they're called haunted.

The ship *Queen Mary* is one such place. It's no ordinary vessel. Visitors have seen slamming doors, felt instant temperature changes, and even heard screams—though no one was there! Is it haunted? Read on to find out *Queen Mary's* spooky history.

THE PARANORMAL AND THE SUPERNATURAL

Events that can't be explained by science are sometimes called paranormal. *Para-* is a prefix from the Greek word for "beyond." So, paranormal describes something that's beyond what we consider normal. Similarly, the prefix *super-* can also mean beyond. So "supernatural" describes something beyond the natural world.

The Queen Mary was once famous for being the best way to travel overseas. Now it's more famous for paranormal reasons.

JOB #534

The *Queen Mary* wasn't always known as a haunted ship. Construction on the vessel began in Scotland in 1930. Owned by Cunard Line, a British-American company, it was built to be a "superliner."

Though the **Great Depression** slowed construction, the ship—then called Job #534—was first launched in 1934. That same year the ship was named. By 1936, the *Queen Mary* was ready for its first voyage. On its sixth journey, it broke a speed record, becoming one of the fastest passenger ships of its day. The *Queen Mary* was soon called the most celebrated ocean liner in the world.

THE NAME

Cunard Line officials told King George V they wanted to name the ship for England's greatest queen, meaning nineteenth-century ruler Queen Victoria. But the king said, "My wife will be delighted that you are naming the ship after her." And so the ship was called the *Queen Mary* instead!

LUXURY LINER

The *Queen Mary* wasn't just fast—it was luxurious. The ship boasted five dining rooms, two swimming pools, a ballroom for dancing, and even a small hospital. Beautiful wood, glass, and marble were used in its construction. **Murals**, paintings, and carvings decorated rooms.

Adding to the **glamour** of the ship were the major Hollywood stars who walked the decks, including Elizabeth Taylor, Audrey Hepburn, Bing Crosby, Fred Astaire, and Clark Gable. World leaders such as Dwight Eisenhower, who traveled on the ship before becoming US president, and British Prime Minister Winston Churchill were also passengers. Churchill sometimes used the *Queen Mary* as an office!

FIRST-CLASS VOYAGE

Have you ever flown first class in a plane? If you have, you know it's very comfortable—and expensive! Passengers pay more for first-class tickets, and they expect what comes with it: good food, more space, and better service. Passengers on the *Queen Mary* bought different class tickets, too, ranging from first to third class.

The Queen Mary's construction was inspired by a style called Art Deco. It featured geometric shapes and bold colors.

THE GREY GHOST

The *Queen Mary* had been carrying passengers for just 3 years when World War II began. The vessel had already proven to be a fast passenger ship. Plus, it had room to carry thousands of people and was ideal for transporting troops.

The outside of the ship was repainted grey—leading to its nickname the "Grey Ghost"—and many of its luxury items were removed. In 1942, the ship reached another record by carrying more than 10,000 people at once. It would soon break this record. In 1943, the *Queen Mary* held its greatest number of passengers: 16,683! Churchill said the ship was invaluable to the war effort.

The Queen Mary *began transporting troops in 1940.*

WAR BRIDES

At the close of World War II, the *Queen Mary* had one more duty. Some American and Canadian soldiers had married European women while they were serving overseas. The *Queen Mary* reunited the families, bringing thousands of women and children to North America.

THE VOYAGE ENDS

The *Queen Mary* was repainted and resumed its regular voyages after World War II. However, the world was changing. New boats offered the latest luxuries such as air conditioning. In 1954, about 1 million people traveled by ship and 600,000 by plane. But by 1965, about 650,000 traveled by ship and 4 million by plane. Airplanes had clearly become the most popular way to travel.

In 1966, Cunard put the *Queen Mary* up for sale. In 1967, Long Beach, California, paid $3.45 million for the ship. The *Queen Mary* took its last **transatlantic** voyage that year. Once docked in Long Beach, it became a museum and a hotel.

THE QUEEN MARY OF LONG BEACH

Long Beach, located near Los Angeles, hoped to attract **tourists** with the ship. Today, the harbor is still a big draw and includes an aquarium, submarine, and several museums. In 2010, the *Queen Mary* got a $5 million makeover. The managing company brought back the glamour of the ship but also added modern luxuries.

Even though it's no longer in service, the Queen Mary has remained one of the most famous ships in the world.

13

A HISTORY OF HAUNTINGS

The once-glamorous ship of the stars became a hero of World War II. So far the history of the *Queen Mary* sounds perfect. So where do the stories of hauntings come from? A sailing vessel often has its share of deaths.

A ship can be dangerous for many reasons, including possible drowning, crashes, and machinery accidents. And ships in wartime are even more dangerous since enemies work to blast them out of the water. At least 49 people died aboard the *Queen Mary* over the years. Yet the ship is said to be home to as many as 150 different spirits! Keep reading to learn some spine-tingling tales.

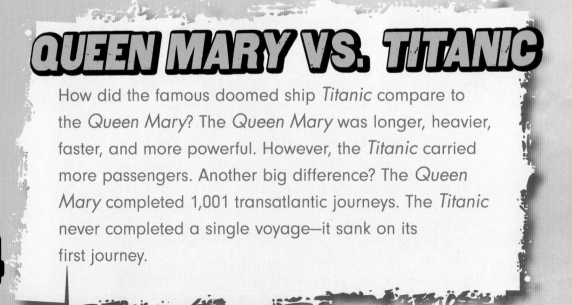

QUEEN MARY VS. TITANIC

How did the famous doomed ship *Titanic* compare to the *Queen Mary*? The *Queen Mary* was longer, heavier, faster, and more powerful. However, the *Titanic* carried more passengers. Another big difference? The *Queen Mary* completed 1,001 transatlantic journeys. The *Titanic* never completed a single voyage—it sank on its first journey.

Dangerous weather can also put ships' passengers in danger.

15

WET FOOTPRINTS

The *Queen Mary* had two swimming pools, one for the first-class passengers and one for those in second class. If you were to peer into the first-class pool room, you might see wet footprints appear on the dry ground. You might hear splashing though no one is around. You may even see women in 1930s-style swimsuits in the pool! All these supernatural events have been reported by pool-room visitors.

In the second-class pool room, some people see the ghost of a little girl named Jackie. It's thought that Jackie drowned in the pool. She doesn't seem to be an unhappy spirit. Many accounts say they hear laughter.

CRYING IN THE PLAYROOM

Just as there were separate swimming pools for passengers with different class tickets, there were separate playrooms for children. People may hear Jackie's laughter in the pool room, but they hear other children crying in the third-class playroom. One crying figure is said to be the ghost of a baby who died on a voyage.

A little girl's voice echoes through the
second-class pool room—but no one's there!

17

WORLD WAR TRAGEDY

As a World War II transport ship, the *Queen Mary* took many soldiers to the front lines of battle—as many as 16,000 at a time. Some of these men and women never returned. This sad fact alone makes people believe they see soldiers walking the deck, perhaps hoping to return to their loved ones. However, one event stands out during the war as the cause of great suffering.

The *Queen Mary* was such an advantage to the **Allies** that German leader Adolf Hitler offered a reward to any captain who could sink it. Therefore, other ships often accompanied the *Queen Mary* to protect it.

THE PSYCHIC SAYS...

Many people believe in the supernatural powers of Peter James. He has even been featured as a **psychic** on TV shows. James has traveled the world exploring haunted places. He named the *Queen Mary* as the most haunted place he had ever been. He's spent a lot of time on the ship and sometimes given tours as well.

Many ships sailed with the Queen Mary *in 1967 on its final journey across the ocean to Long Beach.*

On October 2, 1942, a German **U-boat** was sighted near the *Queen Mary* as it sailed to Scotland. The *Queen Mary* moved in a zigzag motion to avoid being an enemy target.

The small warship guarding the *Queen Mary*, the HMS *Curacao*, cut too close to it. The huge troopship hit the *Curacao*, slicing the warship in two and greatly damaging its own **bow**. Over 300 people died. The *Queen Mary* was under orders not to stop, so the crew couldn't even help the survivors. Other guard ships picked up some men, many of whom died later.

HEARTBREAKING SOUNDS

People have reported hearing strange noises when walking below deck near the *Queen Mary's* bow. The noises sound like metal being crushed. Some even hear men screaming. Could this be the sound of the ship hitting the *Curacao* echoing through time? The sounds have even been caught on tape!

One sailor reported that the Queen Mary *hit the* Curacao, *shown below, "like a knife through butter."*

DOOR 13

Door 13 of the *Queen Mary's* engine room has proven itself to be more than unlucky—it's deadly. The engine room is 50 feet (15 m) below water level. Crews once practiced drills there in case a leak occurred.

In 1966, during one of these drills, 18-year-old John Pedder was killed. He may have been playing a game, jumping back and forth between passages as the door automatically closed. Others say he was trying to squeeze by the door to get a wrench. Either way, the heavy door marked with the number 13 crushed Pedder, killing him.

THE ENGINE ROOM WHERE DOOR 13 IS LOCATED

THE NUMBER 13

Have you ever wondered why the number 13 is unlucky?
Some think it comes from myths. In one **Norse** myth,
the evil god Loki was the thirteenth guest at a great
feast. There he had Balder, the god of joy, killed.
The fear of the number 13 even has a special name:
triskaidekaphobia (trihs-ky-deh-kuh-FOH-bee-uh).

*John Pedder's ghost is one of
the most reported paranormal
sightings on the Queen Mary.*

John Pedder's unfortunate accident isn't the end of the story. After his death, crewmen began seeing a young man who looked like Pedder, bearded and wearing blue overalls, in the hall near door 13. Sometimes the man would ask for his wrench and then disappear before their eyes.

A woman who knew nothing of Pedder's story saw a figure suddenly appear near door 13. Asked later to pick out a photo of the man she had seen, she chose Pedder's photo. Even spookier, people on tours have reported being smeared with grease as they walked through door 13!

IN THE MOVIES

The 1972 movie *The Poseidon Adventure* is about a ship that was overturned, or capsized, by a giant wave. This almost happened to the *Queen Mary* during World War II! Some of the movie was filmed aboard the *Queen Mary*, including a scene in the engine room showing door 13.

John Pedder was the second crewman crushed by door 13, which led to an engine room like this one.

25

POISON!

Senior Second Class Officer William Stark was a navy officer traveling aboard the *Queen Mary* in 1949. One night he decided to pour himself a drink while waiting for some friends to finish work. He grabbed a bottle and poured himself a glass of the clear liquid.

Because he had added lime, it took him a few sips before he realized it wasn't what he thought it was. It turned out the crew was storing a cleaning liquid called tetrachloride in the bottle. Stark laughed about his mistake at first. However, he became sick and was dead 4 days later.

OFFICER IN UNIFORM

Sometimes a man in a white navy uniform is seen walking the main deck. Others have heard choking sounds. Is this William Stark? Some people think hauntings happen where terrible events occur. This would explain why the ghosts of Stark and other unfortunate passengers and crew have appeared on the *Queen Mary*.

This is one of the locations where Officer Stark, the victim of an accidental poisoning, is sometimes seen today.

27

DO YOU BELIEVE?

Now that you've heard about Jackie, John Pedder, the *Curacao*, and William Stark, do you believe—like many others—that the *Queen Mary* is haunted? Remember, some people think there are more than a hundred spirits on this ship! You may want to find one yourself!

The *Queen Mary* is still open to visitors in Long Beach, California, as a hotel and a restaurant, and for tours. Every Halloween, there are spooky mazes and even a costume ball. Halloween would be the perfect time of year for a visit to the world's most haunted ship!

QUEEN MARY 2

The spirit of the *Queen Mary* lives on in another vessel—the *Queen Mary* 2. Also known as the QM2, it's called the most luxurious ocean liner ever built. It has 14 decks, several dining rooms, ballrooms, and even a **planetarium**! There are no hauntings on this ship, though!

People come from all over to see the Queen Mary—and its ghosts!

29

GLOSSARY

Allies: the group of nations, including England and the United States, in World War II that opposed the Axis nations, including Germany and Japan

bow: the front section of a boat

glamour: fashionable appeal

Great Depression: a period of economic troubles with widespread unemployment and poverty (1929–1939)

mural: a large picture painted onto a wall

Norse: relating to ancient Norway

phenomena: events

planetarium: a place with a domed ceiling onto which images of stars, planets, and other space objects are shown to an audience

psychic: a person who claims to have supernatural abilities

tourist: one who visits places far away from home for fun

transatlantic: relating to crossing the Atlantic Ocean

U-boat: a German submarine used during World Wars I and II

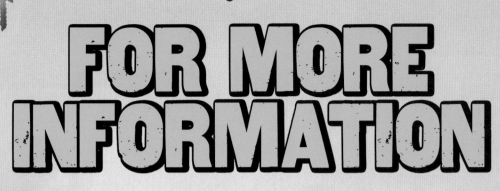

FOR MORE INFORMATION

BOOKS

Belanger, Jeff. *The World's Most Haunted Places*. New York, NY: Rosen Publishing, 2009.

Butler, Daniel Allen. *Warrior Queens: The* Queen Mary *and* Queen Elizabeth *in World War II*. Mechanicsburg, PA: Stackpole Books, 2002.

Ellery, David. *RMS* Queen Mary: *101 Questions and Answers About the Great Transatlantic Liner*. Havertown, PA: Casement Publishing, 2006.

WEBSITES

Ghosts of the Queen Mary in Long Beach
www.legendsofamerica.com/ca-queenmary.html
Read more about the history of the *Queen Mary*—and its spooky passengers!

The Queen Mary
www.queenmary.com
Learn more about the *Queen Mary* and how you can visit it.

INDEX